DECEMBER HOLIDAYS FROM AROUND THE WORLD

Holidays Kids Book
Children's Around the World Books

BABY PROFESSOR
EDUCATION KIDS

Speedy Publishing LLC

40 E. Main St. #1156

Newark, DE 19711

www.speedypublishing.com

Copyright 2017

In this book, we're going to talk about December holidays from around the world. So, let's get right to it!

Every year people around the world look forward to the month of December as a time when they can celebrate with family and friends. Every country has different traditions and, depending on your religion, your holiday will be celebrated with specific spiritual observances as well as festive partying.

Saint Nicholas

ST. NICHOLAS DAY, DECEMBER 6

St. Nicholas Day is not generally known in the United States, but in many European countries it's recognized and celebrated. December 6 in 343 AD is the day that Saint Nicholas died, and this holiday is for remembering this generous man who spent his life giving to others.

Saint Nicholas was a real person and his amazing life became the basis for our iconic Santa Claus. His parents died when he was very young leaving him a sizable inheritance. Although he was now an orphan himself, he began to use his wealth to aid the poor as well as those who were ill. He was a very devout Christian and eventually became a bishop in the city of Myra in what is now part of modern-day Turkey.

Santa Claus

St. Nicholas' Church

One famous legend tells how he helped three impoverished sisters. At that time, when a woman married she had to have a dowry. A dowry was usually a sum of money plus some possessions that she would bring to her husband's house as part of the contract of their marriage.

The sisters were troubled because they knew that since they had no money, their father might be forced to sell them as slaves. Saint Nicholas saved them by secretly going to their house and delivering gold to them, which he placed in their stockings that were hanging to dry above the fireplace. All three girls were able to marry.

Saint Nicholas

The legends and miracles associated with Saint Nicholas continued to grow and although the Reformation in the 1500s frowned upon honoring saints, he remained important in Holland. He was known for protecting children as well as sailors, and he became connected with Christmas gift-giving.

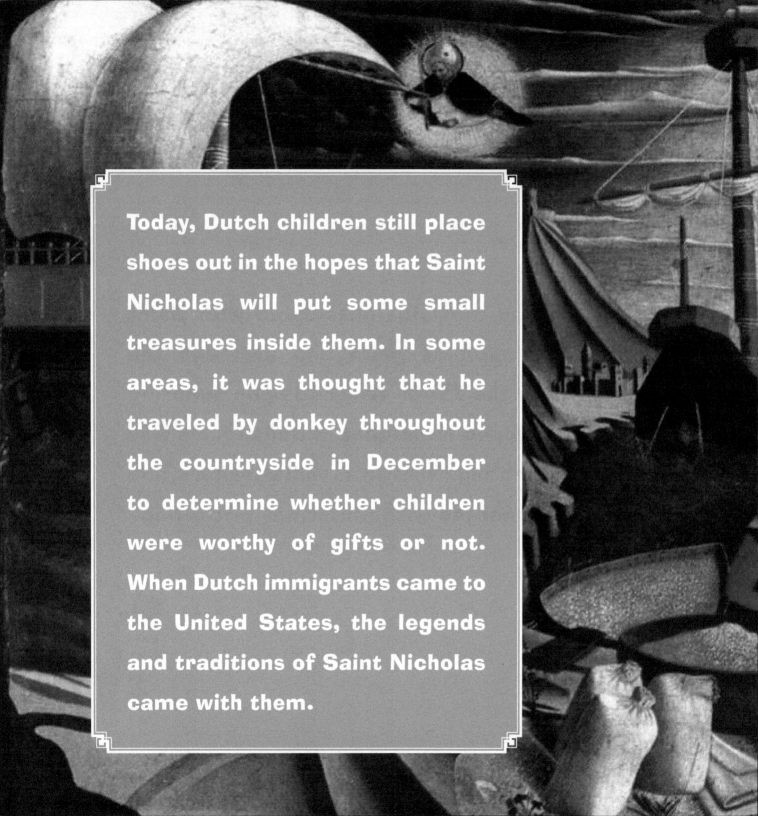

Today, Dutch children still place shoes out in the hopes that Saint Nicholas will put some small treasures inside them. In some areas, it was thought that he traveled by donkey throughout the countryside in December to determine whether children were worthy of gifts or not. When Dutch immigrants came to the United States, the legends and traditions of Saint Nicholas came with them.

St Nicholas saves the ship

Santa Claus and his reindeers

No one knows exactly when the idea of reindeer pulling Santa's sleigh came about, but by the time Clement Clarke Moore created the famous poem "The Night Before Christmas" in 1822, Santa's costume, his reindeer, and his tradition of gift-giving had evolved into an Americanized version of the legend of Saint Nicholas.

CHRISTMAS DAY, DECEMBER 25

Although it's been blended with the legends of Saint Nicholas, Christmas Day, celebrated on December 25 is a celebration of the Feast of the Nativity, which is the birth of Jesus.

Nativity Scene

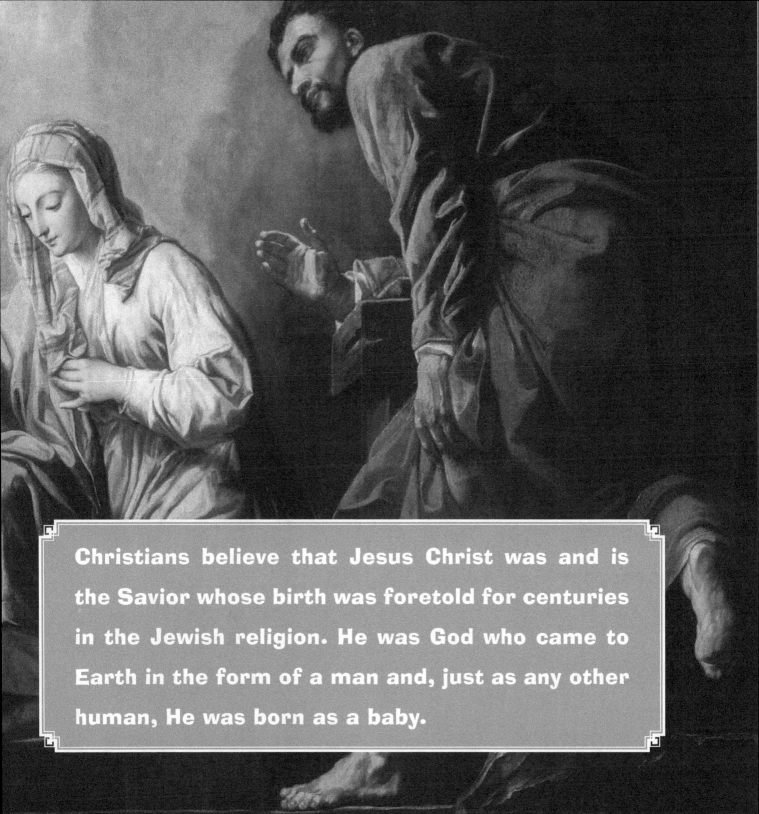

Christians believe that Jesus Christ was and is the Savior whose birth was foretold for centuries in the Jewish religion. He was God who came to Earth in the form of a man and, just as any other human, He was born as a baby.

Mary and Joseph were engaged to be married. The angel Gabriel visited Mary to tell her that she would become pregnant with God's son through a miracle. She was scared, but she was holy and accepted God's word.

When Joseph found out that she was pregnant, he wasn't sure if he should marry her or not. An angel came to him to tell him that Mary was carrying God's son and that he would be Jesus's earthly father. Mary and Joseph traveled to Bethlehem from Nazareth for a census.

When they got there, there was no place for them to stay so they found shelter in a stable and Mary gave birth to Jesus, wrapped him tightly in a long cloth, and placed him in a manger. When Jesus grew up, He died on a cross so that the sins of mankind could be forgiven and that mankind could be saved and be given everlasting life.

Nativity Scene

Over two billion Christians celebrate Christmas around the world. Even non-Christians get into the spirit. There are special masses or services and other religious ceremonies. There are Nativity scenes in churches and in people's yards.

Most homes have a decorated Christmas tree, people sing Christmas carols, and they eat special meals with traditional food from their country as they rejoice with their families and friends. It's a time for gift-giving, especially for children who can't wait for Christmas morning to see what Santa has brought them. Retailers around the world have promoted Christmas heavily so that people will buy lots of gifts and retail stores will reap the profits.

Boxing Day

BOXING DAY, DECEMBER 26

This holiday is popular in Great Britain as well as in the country of Canada. It's also celebrated in Australia and in New Zealand. During Christmas Day, the servants that were working in the manors of the British aristocracy had to work. However, their employers prepared special boxes for them, which they took home to open the next day since they were off work.

Another theory about the origins of Boxing Day is that churches had boxes where people donated alms and money for the poor. The biggest collections for these boxes were on Christmas when people were feeling the most generous. The day after Christmas, the boxes were distributed so that the less fortunate could have a Christmas holiday too.

In the United Kingdom, Boxing Day is a time when there are football matches as well as horse racing. In the countries that celebrate Boxing Day, it's also a time when stores put a lot of merchandise on sale, similar to Black Friday in the United States.

HANUKKAH, EIGHT DAYS BASED ON THE LUNAR CALENDAR

Hanukkah is a Jewish festival, also known as The Festival of Lights. It lasts for eight full days and begins on the 25th day of the month of Kislev. The Jewish people use a different calendar. It is a lunar calendar so the month of Kislev can begin any time from the last part of November to late in December on the Gregorian calendar, which is the calendar we use in the United States.

Hanukkah Menorah

Persecution by Antiochus

The reason for the holiday goes back to 165 BC. At that time, a Greek ruler called Antiochus wanted to outlaw the Jewish religion. He took over the Jewish temple, their most sacred place. Three years later the Jewish people were able to take their temple back, but they needed to purify and cleanse the temple so that it could once again be used for their worship.

A special menorah is used for Hanukkah. Instead of 6 candles with a 7th candle in the center, this special menorah is called a hanukkiyah, which has 8 candles with a 9th candle for the center. The 9th candle is known as the "shammash." This servant candle is used to light the others.

Jewish Holiday Hanukkah

Jewish Holiday Hanukkah

It is in the center of the hanukkiyah and is considered to have a higher position. On the first night, the family lights one candle, on the second night two candles, and so on until all eight candles have been lit on the last night of Hanukkah.

The candles are lit moving from the left side to the right side. A special thank you blessing is offered to God and a hymn in honor of the holiday is sung by all. The hanukkiyah is placed in the window to remind others of the holiday's significance.

Colorful Dreidels

Gift-giving is part of Hanukkah as well. Gifts are given on each night and games are played. One of the most popular games uses a dreidel. It's a top that has four sides. The letters on each side stand for the phrase "Nes Gadol Hayah Po," which translates to "a great miracle happened here."

Here are the rules of the game:

- If the letter for "n" comes up, nothing happens.

- If the letter for "g" comes up the player wins what's in the pot, which might be a coin or a nut or a piece of chocolate.

- If the letter "h" comes up the player wins half of what's in the pot.

- If the letter is "p" comes up, then the player has to put something else in the pot and the next person spins.

Dreidel

Potato Pancakes

Interesting foods are eaten during Hanukkah as well, such as potato pancakes called latkes and deep-fried doughnuts filled with jam and sprinkled with sugar.

KWANZAA, DECEMBER 26 THROUGH JANUARY 1st

Kwanzaa come from a word in Swahili that translates to "first harvest fruits." It was established in 1966 by Maulana Karenga. He was a professor of African-American studies and a bestselling author.

Kwanzaa

The idea behind the holiday was to offer African-Americans a way to celebrate their African heritage and to promote a feeling of unity, purpose, and faith. Kwanzaa is celebrated over seven days and a candle is lit within a candelabra for each of seven abiding principles.

Awesome! Now you know more about December holidays around the world. You can find more Around the World books from Baby Professor by searching the website of your favorite book retailer.

Holiday Celebration

Printed in the USA
CPSIA information can be obtained
at www.ICGtesting.com
LVHW071046211123
764451LV00025B/510